OTHER GIFTBOOKS IN THIS SERIES

mum	*baby girl!*	*happy day!*
dad	*baby boy!*	*hope! dream!*
son	*love*	*friend*

Printed simultaneously in 2007 by Helen Exley Giftbooks in Great Britain and Helen Exley Giftbooks LLC in the USA.

12 11 10 9 8 7 6 5 4 3 2 1

Illustrations © Joanna Kidney 2007
Copyright © Helen Exley 2007
Text copyright – see page 94.
The moral right of the author has been asserted.

ISBN 13: 978-1-84634-007-9

A copy of the CIP data is available from the British Library on request.

Edited by Helen Exley
Pictures by Joanna Kidney

Printed in China

Helen Exley Giftbooks, 16 Chalk Hill, Watford, Herts WD19 4BG, UK.
Helen Exley Giftbooks LLC, 185 Main Street, Spencer MA 01562, USA.
www.helenexleygiftbooks.com

A HELEN EXLEY GIFTBOOK

daughter!

PICTURES BY JOANNA KIDNEY

A tiny daughter
gives parents a life
in a climate of
perpetual wonder.

PIERRE DOUCET

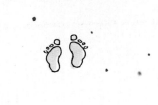

I wanted to change the world overnight,
    to make it a safer, easier, better place
for this miniature woman,
        this receptacle of all my dreams
                and aspirations....

MICHELE GUINNESS,
FROM "TAPESTRY OF VOICES"

You are our gift to the future.

A light, a hope, a promise.

PAM BROWN, B.1928

...they bring their special charm
into the world, a delight in detail,
a tenderness in relationship,
a sensitivity to joy and sorrow
and spiritual truth.

MICHELE GUINNESS,
FROM "TAPESTRY OF VOICES"

Daughters do wonderful things.
Not the wonderful things
you expected them to do.
Different things.
Astonishing things.
Better than you ever dreamed.

MARION C. GARRETTY

I am hers to be with,
and hope to be what she needs,
and know of no reason
why I should ever desert her.

LAURIE LEE (1914–1997)

...my happiness is my daughter,
who is pretty and smart
and laughing
– and who is my friend.

JOAN RIVERS, B.1933, FROM "STILL TALKING"

"Thank heavens for little girls"...
With pigtails and pony tails,
in jeans and party dresses,
climbing trees,
reading books,
sucking gobstoppers
and turning cartwheels....

MICHELE GUINNESS,
FROM "TAPESTRY OF VOICES"

...she sings,
long notes from the belly or the throat,
Her legs kick her feet up to her nose,
She rests
– laid still like a large rose.
She is our child....

JENNIFER ARMITAGE, FROM "TO OUR DAUGHTER"

I would tear down a star
and put it into a smart jewelry box
if I could.
I would seal up love
in a long thin bottle
so that you could sip it
whenever it was needed
if I could.

ANNE SEXTON (1928–1974),
IN A LETTER TO HER DAUGHTER, LINDA, 1974

Thank you for the chance

to rediscover the world.

PAMELA DUGDALE

You stormed into our lives
like a tornado.
You toddled over all our plans.
You screamed through
our best-loved movies.
You threw up on everything.
You made our lives wonderful.

STUART AND LINDA MACFARLANE

Nothing could give me
greater happiness than when

hear her throaty little laugh
or see her
clapping her hands
in delight.

ANNA PASTERNAK,
FROM "DAILY MAIL", OCTOBER 19, 2004

Wrapped round
her little finger?!
           Not at all!!
I wanted to buy her
         all those teddies,
dolls, books....

STUART MACFARLANE, B.1953

I told myself that when
[my daughters] were twenty-one
I'd stop worrying.
I didn't.
Then I said when they got married
I'd stop worrying.
I didn't.
Now all this worrying
is starting to worry me.

LEE IACOCCA, B.1924

Teaching your daughter to drive
requires great patience
and understanding.
Fortunately my daughter has both.

STUART MACFARLANE, B.1953

When no one can get through
to anyone by phone or e-mail
there are daughters in the house.

PAM BROWN, B.1928

If the phone's not engaged
the bathroom is.

AMANDA BELL

You fill our lives
with bills,
taxi fares,
worries,
loud music...
but most of all
you fill our lives
with love.

STUART AND LINDA
MACFARLANE

Arthur always had his arms around
his daughter Camera.
When he talked about her,
his face would light up
like stars in the sky.
He showed more feeling
for his daughter than I had seen him
show his whole life.

HORACE ASHE, UNCLE OF ARTHUR ASHE

She holds out her hand to air,
Sea, sky, wind, sun,
movement, stillness.
And wants to hold them all.
My finger is her earth connection, me,
and earth.

JENNIFER ARMITAGE, FROM "TO OUR DAUGHTER"

There are things
I cannot heal with a hug.
Grown up matters beyond my skills.
I wish I had some magic
that could make such things come right.
All I can do is be here.
Always.

PAM BROWN, B.1928

My love will be with you
When life's woes weigh you down.

My love will be with you
When life is fearful.

My love will be with you
Today and forever.

STUART MACFARLANE, B.1953

Sometimes,
when you were a little baby,
I would get up
in the middle of the night
just to look at you....

STUART MACFARLANE, B.1953

I keep an album of photographs of you
– as if I could hold on
to all the different yous –

But they don't really matter.
Because every time I see you
I think "This is the best time."

PAM BROWN, B.1928

WORDS AREN'T ENOUGH
TO DESCRIBE THE DELIGHT...
MY CHILDREN HAVE GIVEN ME
THE GREATEST HAPPINESS
IN MY LIFE.

IMRAN KHAN, B.1952

When all the world is dreary,
I think about my daughter

her brightness and her laughter,
and life comes right again.

PAM BROWN, B.1928

...the joy and pride I've taken
in both my daughters
has never wavered,
and has simply increased over time.

ARNOLD PALMER, B.1929,
FROM "A GOLFER'S LIFE"

I have a beautiful daughter,
golden like a flower

my beloved Cleïs, for her,
in her place,
I would not accept
the whole of Lydia....

SAPPHO, C.650 B.C.

I recall a time in my life
during which I was in severe emotional pain.
One morning I woke up to find
my thirteen-year-old daughter
sleeping on the floor beside my bed.
When I questioned her about this
she quietly told me
that she wanted to be near me
because she knew I was hurting....

BARBARA THOMAS

My real treasures
are inside an old baby milk tin.
Your first shoes,
a lock of hair from your first haircut,
your first drawing....

LINDA MACFARLANE, B.1953

What I have learned
in the process of raising (four) daughters
...is that there is no single answer,
no magic formula,
no rigid set of guidelines...
There is love.

GEORGE LEONARD

One moment in diapers
the next in jeans.
From crawling to driving
in an instance.
Time disappeared so quickly.
Yet, I am blessed
to have shared it with you.

STUART MACFARLANE, B.1953

Within minutes,
we're pedaling away,
the two of us,
a genetic sewing machine
that runs on limitless love.

It's my belief that....
there is a kind of blood-hyphen that is,
finally, indissoluble.

CAROL SHIELDS, FROM "SWANN"

I never thought I could love so much
or hurt so badly for another person.

JENNIFER TO KALLYSTA,
FROM "LETTERS TO OUR DAUGHTERS"

When I look into your eyes

feel mine shine with love.

LINDA MACFARLANE, B.1953

Jill gives so much back to me.
I value her maturity and her insight.
She is my confidante.
Not only my daughter
but my good friend.

ADAH ASKEW,
FROM "MOTHERS AND DAUGHTERS"

There is nothing,
absolutely nothing
that can cheer up
a dismal evening
more successfully
than a phone call
from a daughter.

PAM BROWN, B.1928

The loving, happy aspects
come mostly from the girl's freshness,
her curiosity, her openness,
her irresponsibility,
her exuberance (despite all pressures),
her affection, her loyalty,
her sympathy, her gentleness,
her wide-eyed enjoyment...

RACHEL BILLINGTON, B.1942,
FROM "THE GREAT UMBILICAL"

Walk gently my daughter
Through life's joys, songs and triumphs.
For my love will be there in your heart.
Walk gently my daughter
Through life's sorrows, pains and woes...
Walk gently my daughter
Through all life's great mysteries.
For my love will be there in your heart.

LINDA MACFARLANE, B.1953

It was a joy to see you grow
– but a sadness too
    – for you found your independence
        and no longer needed me.
    But now I see
        that the years have given
more than they have taken
    – and I celebrate my daughter
        and my friend.

PAM BROWN, B.1928

You can go without regret
        Away from this
familiar land,
        Leaving your kiss
                upon my hair
And all the future
        in your hands.

MARGARET MEAD (1901–1978)

I'm proud of all
your achievements.

But I'm most proud of you

being just you.

You are special to me
whatever you do.

PAM BROWN, B.1928

I have done little with my life,
created nothing wonderful,
given no new knowledge to the world.
But I am content.
I have given it a daughter.
Most wonderful.
Most wise.

MAYA V. PATEL, B.1943

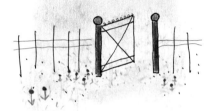

A Child of Happiness
always seems like an old soul
    living in a new body,
and her face is very serious
until she smiles,
and then the sun lights up
    the world....

ANNE CAMERON,
FROM "DAUGHTERS OF COPPER WOMAN"

Little Girl
My Stringbean,
My Lovely Woman.

ANNE SEXTON (1928–1974)

Helen Exley runs her own publishing company which sells giftbooks in more than seventy countries. She had always wanted to do a little book on smiles, and had been collecting the quotations for many years, but always felt that the available illustrations just weren't quite right. Helen fell in love with Joanna Kidney's happy, bright pictures and knew immediately they had the feel she was looking for. She asked Joanna to work on *smile*, and then to go on to contribute the art for four more books: *friend, happy day!, love* and *hope! dream!* We have now published nine more books in this series, which are selling in 27 languages.

Joanna Kidney lives in County Wicklow in Ireland. She juggles her time between working on various illustration projects, producing her own art for shows and exhibitions and looking after her baby boy. Her whole range of greeting cards, *Joanna's Pearlies* – some of which appear in this book – won the prestigious Henries oscar for 'best fun or graphic range'.